THE BUILD A BAG BOOK

Tote Bags

Debbie Shore

SEARCH PRESS

First published in 2018

Search Press Limited
Wellwood, North Farm Road,
Tunbridge Wells, Kent TN2 3DR

Reprinted 2018, 2019, 2020

Illustrations and text copyright © Debbie Shore 2018

Photographs copyright © Garie Hind 2018

Design copyright © Search Press Ltd. 2018

ISBN: 978-1-78221-618-6

The Publishers and author can accept no responsibility
for any consequences arising from the information,
advice or instructions given in this publication.

Suppliers
If you have difficulty in obtaining any of the materials and
equipment mentioned in this book, then please visit the
Search Press website for details of suppliers:
www.searchpress.com

For further inspiration:

- join the Half Yard Sewing Club:
www.halfyardsewingclub.com

- visit Debbie's YouTube channel:
www.youtube.com/user/thimblelane

- visit Debbie's website:
www.debbieshoresewing.com

ACKNOWLEDGEMENTS

This is for Mum, not for
encouraging me to sew, but
for passing on her drawing and
mathematical skills, both of which
help when designing bags!

THE BUILD A BAG BOOK

Tote Bags

Sew 15 stunning projects and endless variations

For those of you who
can't have enough bags,
in every colour and style for any
occasion! For those who like to
make a statement, be different,
unique and classy. Enjoy!

DEDICATION

CONTENTS

INTRODUCTION

The tote is such a versatile bag that can be useful for work, evenings out, weekends away and, of course, for everyday use, which is why I'm so excited to bring you this book! Using the two plastic templates provided you can create the 15 tote bag designs I've included, and then use the templates over and over again to mix and match and create your own unique designs (there's advice on how to do this on pages 92–93).

The templates include options for a wide or narrow squared-off bag base, a bag flap, patch pockets to use on the outside or inside of your bag, handles, a bow, a zipped panel for a secure lining and a zipped pocket for the outside, inside or indeed both! Simply draw around the templates onto your fabric and cut – no pins required! The templates are semi-transparent to enable fussy cutting, and are easy to store and wipe clean.

If you are a complete beginner, start with the basic tote, a no-frills, no-closures and no-trimmings bag (see pages 30–33) that any skill level of sewer should be able to create in just a little time. Then it's up to you if you want to add a bag base, feet, fastenings and hardware. I always think these add a shop-bought look to your bag, so instructions on fitting the most popular types are included.

Whatever fabric and colours you choose, you'll be able to create unique, stylish and purposeful tote bags with ease, using the templates to enable you to become a bag designer for yourself!

Use a 5mm (¼in) seam allowance unless otherwise stated – this is included in your template measurements.

Debbie
x

See pages 74–77.

See pages 58–61.

See pages 82–87.

This is a simple tote with a squared-off base but no pockets or fastenings. It features a quilted design, and is a great way to use up your button stash! See pages 70–73.

UNDERSTANDING THE TEMPLATES

Your templates are semi-transparent so that you can place them over a particular area of your fabric to fussy cut a pattern if you wish; they are also wipe-clean and easy to store flat. Use an erasable ink pen or chalk pencil to draw your chosen outline.

SELECTING THE TEMPLATES

Whenever you need to use a template, your project instructions will clearly tell you which one to use, and show the template with the relevant parts highlighted, as shown below – here you can see the templates required are the tote shape with large cut-out corners from template 1, and the curved flap shape from template 2. Some of the pieces will need to be cut on the fold of the fabric, so you will need to place your template on the fold where indicated; see below.

Template 1

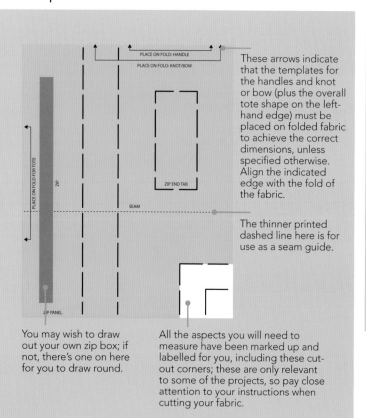

These arrows indicate that the templates for the handles and knot or bow (plus the overall tote shape on the left-hand edge) must be placed on folded fabric to achieve the correct dimensions, unless specified otherwise. Align the indicated edge with the fold of the fabric.

The thinner printed dashed line here is for use as a seam guide.

You may wish to draw out your own zip box; if not, there's one on here for you to draw round.

All the aspects you will need to measure have been marked up and labelled for you, including these cut-out corners; these are only relevant to some of the projects, so pay close attention to your instructions when cutting your fabric.

Template 2

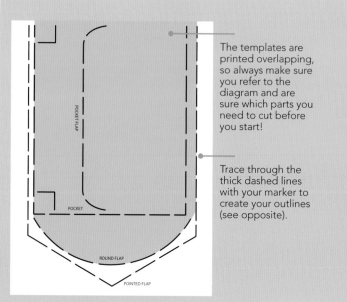

The templates are printed overlapping, so always make sure you refer to the diagram and are sure which parts you need to cut before you start!

Trace through the thick dashed lines with your marker to create your outlines (see opposite).

USING THE TEMPLATES

1 Refer to the pattern pieces needed for each style of bag. Where indicated, place the template over the fold of your fabric as shown right.

2 Then simply draw through the slots in your template to mark the outline of your bag or flap pieces.

3 Mark in any cut-out corners, if needed.

4 Cut out as many pieces as required, following the drawn dashed lines.

5 If you need to add a zip, draw around the inside of the zip box, or draw freehand to the size you need.

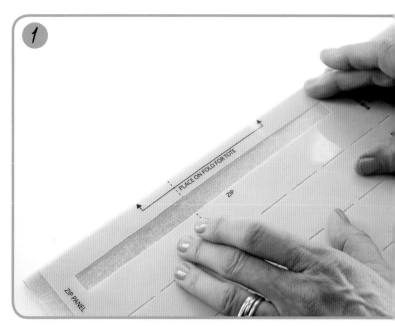

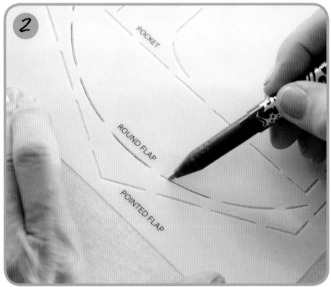

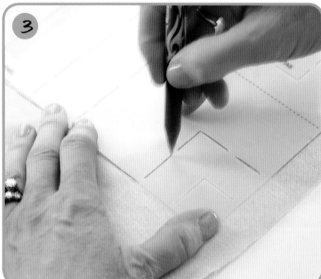

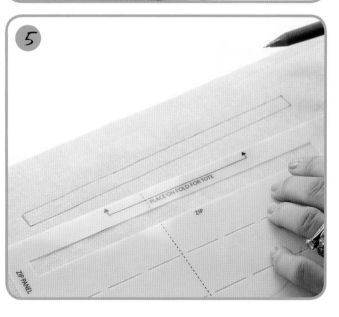

This cute embroidered tote features a curved flap that fastens with a magnetic snap fastener, as well as a squared-off base. See pages 38–41.

Add a stylish touch to a tote by creating a large decorative bow in a complementary colour. This bag also features a zipped lining for extra security. See pages 42–45.

MATERIALS

1. FABRICS

When I'm sewing bags, I choose the colour and pattern of fabric I like, then worry about the fibre content later. The perfect weight for a bag is upholstery fabric – the kind you'd use for curtains – a heavy woven cotton that is durable but is still easy to sew. However, **cotton (1a)** is a favourite of mine. If it is too lightweight, add fusible fleece or interfacing to the wrong side to add rigidity (see opposite). This is imperative if you're using stretch fabric, as you don't want a bouncy bag!

Create a more casual look with **corduroy (1b)** or **denim (1c)** (or both!). If you choose **laminated fabric (1d)**, a non-stick presser foot for your sewing machine will help to feed the coated fabric through more easily.

I don't pre-wash the fabric I use for bag making as it's unlikely to need to be laundered and I like the starchy, crisp feel of new fabrics. Most bags can be spot-cleaned, but spray with fabric protector if you wish, to guard against stains.

1a

1b

1c

1d

2. FABRIC SUPPORT

Most of the fabrics I use for bag making need a little support to give them rigidity and form. I generally use **fusible fleece**, which is a 3mm (⅛in) thick polyester padding with adhesive dots on one side that fuse the fleece to the wrong side of the fabric when ironed. (Refer to the manufacturer's instructions, as some need steam and some don't.)

Interfacing (2a) is either woven or non-woven iron-on stabilizer, available in different weights, from a fine sheet that can prevent knit fabrics from stretching or loose-weave fabrics from twisting, to a leather-like material that will produce quite a stiff bag. I would avoid the latter if you are a new sewer, as it can be quite difficult to work with. Experiment with different weights of interfacing: if you buy from a shop, you will have an idea of how firm your fabric will be when you feel the interfacing and see how it drapes.

Wadding or batting (2b) (same thing!) can also be used to give a softer feel to your bag, and is available in a wide range of natural and man-made fibres. Use spray fabric adhesive if you wish to secure it to the back of your fabric before sewing.

Foam stabilizer is an excellent choice for larger bags; this is a 5mm (¼in) thick foam that will allow your tote to stand up unaided. Buy either sew-in or single-sided fusible versions. I've used this for my crafty tote on pages 34–37. Trim it back to the seams to make it easier to sew.

For most of the projects in this book I've kept it simple by using fusible fleece throughout, whether I've used upholstery fabric or craft cotton to create my totes. The exception is laminated fabric or faux leather, which can't be ironed from the right side. In these cases I would adhere the fleece with repositionable spray fabric adhesive.

3. THREADS

It's important to use good-quality thread when making bags to achieve the strongest seams. After all, when you've gone to the expense of buying beautiful fabric and spent your precious time making a bag, you don't want your seams to let you down! A quality thread will be smooth and not fibrous; don't use old or inexpensive thread. If in doubt, do the tug test: if you yank the thread from the spool and it snaps easily, it's likely also to snap when sewing.

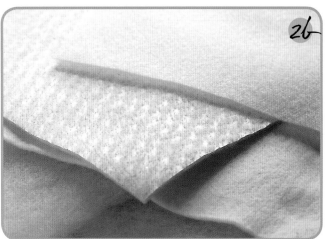

TOOLS

1. SEWING MACHINE

Although you'll mainly be using a straight stitch, your bag fabric could be quite heavy, so you may need a machine that has the power to push the needle through the material. I'd always recommend a computerized machine as they are feature-packed and easy to use; choose a big brand that comes with a warranty and customer support. Buy a few denim needles, too – these are strong needles that will easily slip through thick or tough fabrics.

2. PRESSER FEET

Your machine will have standard, buttonhole and zipper feet for most of your sewing needs, but it is worth investing in a walking foot to help sew through multiple layers of fabrics to prevent them slipping, a darning foot (shown) for free-motion embroidery, and a non-stick foot for laminates.

3. SHEARS

Dressmaking shears with angled handles make cutting straight lines and multiple layers a breeze.

4. SMALL SCISSORS

Embroidery scissors are useful for snipping small threads and buttonholes.

5. PINKING SHEARS

The serrated blades on pinking shears cut at small 45-degree angles to prevent woven fabric from fraying. They are a terrific way of finishing seams and also useful for cutting quickly into curved areas, such as a bag flap.

6. ROTARY CUTTER, RULER AND CUTTING MAT

These three tools go hand in hand to make light work of cutting accurately. Choose the largest self-healing mat you have room for. A 45mm (1¾in) rotary cutter is the most used but a 60mm (2⅜in) one makes it easier to cut through multiple layers of fabric and wadding/batting. A 61cm (24in) rectangular ruler with 45-degree markings is also useful for cutting on the bias.

7. TAILOR'S HAM

These are sawdust-filled shapes that are pushed inside your bag to enable you to press the seams without pressing your bag flat, while also keeping your hands out of the way of a hot iron!

8. MARKING TOOLS

To draw around your templates you'll need some form of marking pen. I use erasable ink pens, whereby the ink disappears either by the heat of an iron, with water or fades away over the course of a few hours. Beware of ironing over water- or air-erasable ink, as the heat can make the ink permanent! I would advise that you only use the heat-erasable pens in the seam allowances, as they may mark your fabric. Fabric or chalk pencils are also a good option – simply brush away the markings when they're not needed any more.

9. ADHESIVES

A tacking/basting glue stick offers a quick way of holding seams together before sewing. I use these to secure zips instead of hand-tacking/basting to save time. Repositionable spray fabric adhesives are an excellent choice for bonding wadding/batting to the wrong side of your fabrics. Permanent adhesives in wet glue form are strong enough to secure embellishments to your bag, while spray adhesives make light work of appliqué.

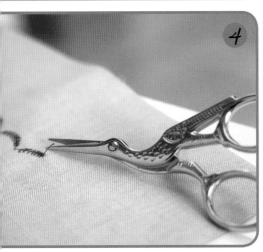

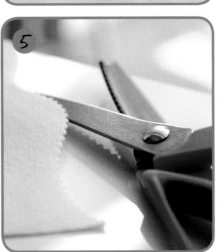

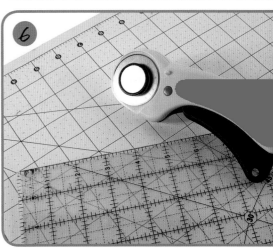

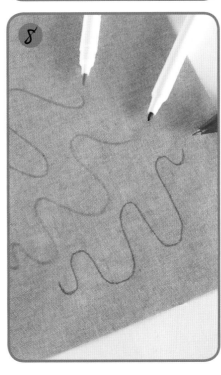

TECHNIQUES

ZIPPED PANEL

This zipped closure can be fitted into any of your totes for added security.

Using your template

To complete this technique you will need to use the zip panel outline and the zip end tab on TEMPLATE 1.

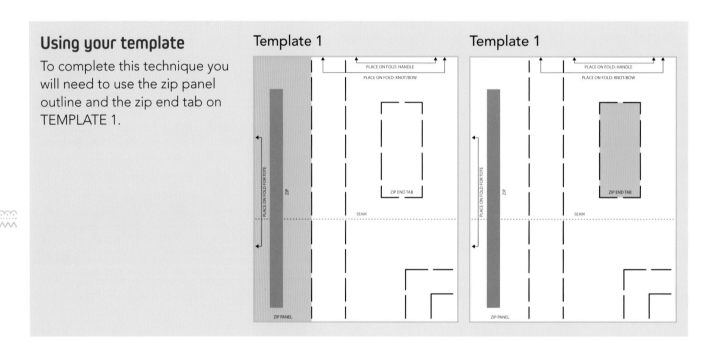

1 Cut four strips of fabric using the zip panel markings on your template (as indicated above).

2 Cut two pieces of fabric using the zip end tab markings on your template (as indicated above).

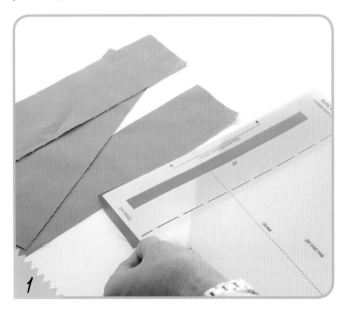

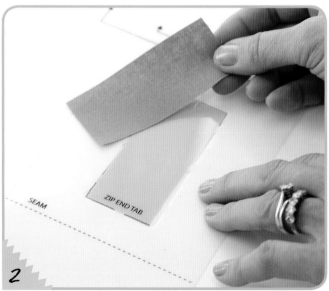

3

4

5

6

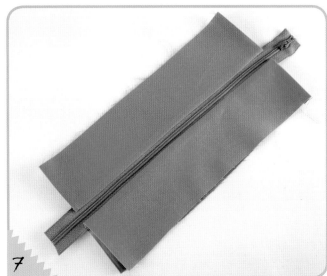

7

3 Take the two zip tab pieces and press the short ends of each piece over, wrong sides together, by 5mm (¼in), as shown.

4 Fold the strip in half so that the raw edges are on the outside and sew along both sides. Snip off the corners.

5 Turn right side out and press.

6 Take the four long strips, fold the short ends to the wrong sides by 5mm (¼in) and press. It may help to hold the fabric by using a fabric glue stick inside the folds.

7 Sew a strip of fabric right sides together to each side of the zip, then press open. Sew the remaining two pieces to the opposite sides of the zip tape so that the zip is sandwiched in between. Trim the zip to make it 5cm (2in) longer than the fabric at each end. I've used a continuous zip, but if you use a standard zip and the ends are now open, hand-sew them together.

8

8 Roll one side of the zip panel towards the zip, then fold the remaining two pieces over the zip to bring the raw edges right sides together and pin.

9 Sew along the edge, being careful not to sew through the rolled fabric within. Remove the pins.

10 Turn the right side out: this may be a struggle but it will work! Repeat the rolling, folding and turning process with the other side of the zip.

11 Dab a little glue over the ends of the zip, then pop on the tabs. Top-stitch around the tabs.

12 To fit the zipped panel into the lining of your tote, measure and mark a line 5cm (2in) from the top right side of a lining piece.

13 Sew the zipped panel, zip facing upwards, centrally along this line.

14 Repeat with the second side of the lining, and you're ready to sew the zipped lining into your tote!

FABRIC STRAPS/HANDLES

There are two types of fabric handle for you to make in this book: open-ended and closed-ended. The open-ended handles are sewn into the top seams of your bag, the closed-ended handles are sewn to the front of your bag.

Add interfacing or fusible fleece to the wrong side of your fabric strips if you need a stiffer handle, or give them a blast of spray starch for a crisp finish. You can make the handles shorter if needed just by cutting off some of the length, or extend them by elongating the template.

Open-ended strap/handle

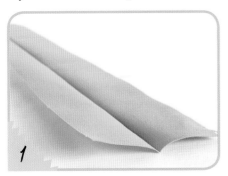
1

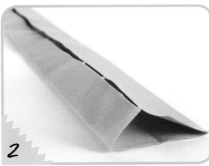

2

3

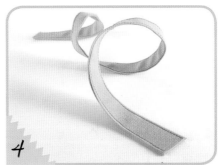
4

1 Cut out your fabric as per the instructions in your project, using the template. Fold the fabric in half lengthways and press.

2 Open out the fabric, fold the two long sides to the centre and press again.

3 Fold the whole handle in half again and press.

4 Top-stitch along both long sides of your handle to complete. Your handle is now ready to insert into the seams of your bag.

Closed-ended strap/handle

Follow steps 1–3 as above.

4 Fold the long sides of the handle together so that the raw edges are on the outside. Sew across the bottom.

5 Turn right side out, then top-stitch all around the edge.

4

5

ZIPPED POCKET

I call this a 'letterbox' zip, as the opening reminds me of a letterbox and the lining fabric is 'posted' through the hole. I use it to create pockets in bag linings, and this is what I'm showing here, but you could also use this technique on the outer fabric of a bag. I prefer to use continuous zipping, as it can be cut to the size you need.

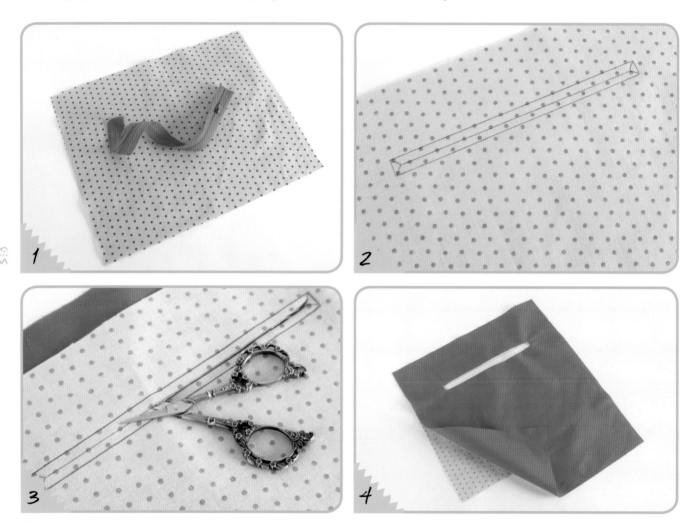

1 Cut two pieces of pocket lining fabric to the size of the pocket you need. This should be shorter than your bag lining fabric, and can either be the same width, so that the pocket is sewn into the side seam, or narrower than the bag. Choose a zip that is 2.5–5cm (1–2in) longer than the pocket opening – it will sit flatter when the ends (with the metal stoppers) are cut off – or cut a length of continuous zipping to size.

2 Draw a rectangle onto the wrong side of one pocket lining piece in the position you'd like the zip, measuring 1cm (½in) wide, and the length of the zip opening; use your template to help you draw this. Draw another line straight through the centre of the box, with a 'Y' shape at each end going into the corners of the rectangle.

3 Pin this right sides together to your bag lining fabric. With a small stitch on your machine, carefully sew around the box. Take a small, sharp pair of scissors and cut along the centre line, then into the 'Y' shape up to, but not through, the stitches. Remove the pins.

4 Push the lining through the hole, and press.

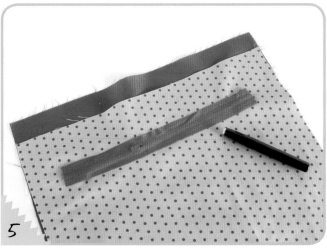

5 Place the zip behind the hole with the teeth facing down, as shown. Either tack/baste or use a temporary glue stick to hold the zip in place. Sew around the edge of the zip on your machine using a zipper foot; move the zip head out of the way as you sew round, to avoid wiggly stitch lines.

6 Pin the two pocket pieces right sides together, keeping the bag lining out of the way. If your pocket is going to fit into the side seam (as shown in steps 6a and 6b), sew across the top and bottom of the pocket. Then, tack/baste the pocket to the side of the lining. Remove the pins. Alternatively, if your pocket is narrower than the width of the lining, sew all the way around the two pocket pieces, avoiding sewing through the bag lining fabric (see 6c).

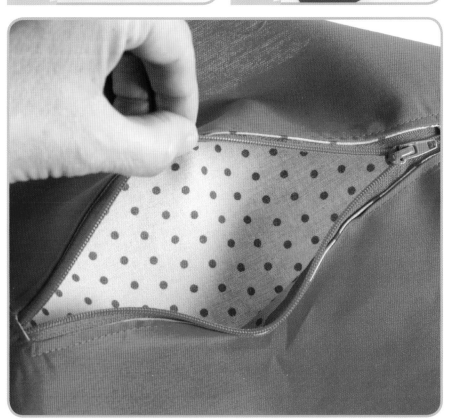

The finished zipped pocket.

PIPING

A strip of piping around a bag or across a pocket gives a professional finishing touch to your work, and is simple to make yourself. Cord comes in many assorted widths; I'd use a fine cord on pockets, and up to 5mm (¼in) wide cord for the bag seams.

 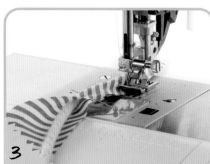 

1 Cut your fabric into strips that are wide enough to wrap around the cord and go under the sewing-machine needle. If you're taking the piping around corners and curves, cut the fabric strips on the bias; if your piping is sewn into a straight seam, such as for the piped tote on pages 50–53, then you can cut on the straight grain.

2 Pin the raw edges together, wrong sides facing, sandwiching the cord in the centre.

3 With the zipper foot on your machine, sew alongside the cord, making sure the raw edges of the strip are together. Take out the pins as you sew.

4 To apply the piping, sandwich it between the two pieces of fabric, right sides and raw edges together, then sew with your zipper foot. (Piping feet are available for some sewing machines.) If you're a beginner, you may find it easier to sew the piping to one side of the fabric at a time.

FUSSY CUTTING

This is a method of cutting out a particular part of the pattern on your fabric; for instance, if you wanted to feature a specific part of the design on a pocket or flap. As your templates are semi-transparent, simply place them over the area you wish to cut, trace around the pattern and cut!

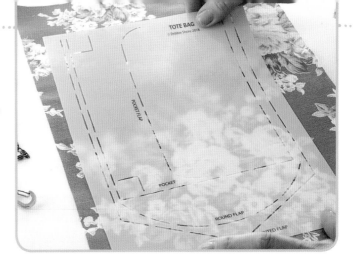

MAGNETIC SNAP FASTENERS

These simple-to-fit clasps don't usually come with instructions, so this is how to fit them. I'd recommend placing a scrap of fabric behind the clasp, on the wrong side of your fabric, to stabilize the fabric and help to stop the clasp pulling. The clasps come in two parts with a disc-shaped back section for each side. If you're fitting the clasp to a bag with a flap, the thinner part of the clasp will go onto the flap and the thicker section onto the bag.

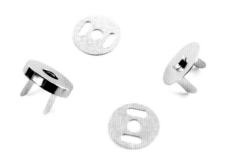

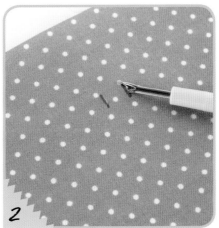

1 Mark the position of the clasp with an erasable ink pen, by taking the back of the clasp and marking through the two long holes either side of the centre.

2 Take your seam ripper or a small pair of sharp scissors, and make a small incision over the long lines. It's better to make the cuts too small so they can be made bigger; if you cut them too big, you may ruin your project.

3 Push the prongs of the clasps through the holes.

4 Open out the prongs on the back of the fabric. It doesn't really matter whether you open them outwards or close them inwards, but I find them easier to open outwards as shown.

BIAS BINDING

Adding bias binding around the top and flap of a bag gives a neat finish, and if you make your own, you know you'll always have the right colour to match your bag perfectly. Bias tape is a strip of fabric cut on the diagonal, at a 45-degree angle, which allows a little 'give' so the fabric stretches around curves without puckering, making it perfect for the curve of a flap. To cut your fabric accurately you'll need a rotary cutter, rectangular ruler and cutting mat. Cutters of 45mm or 60mm are the most popular sizes, and the bigger the ruler and mat the better.

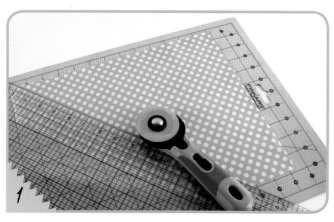

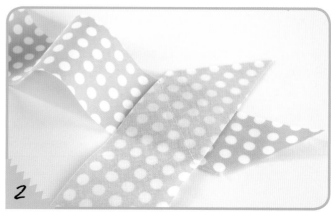

1 Lay your fabric squarely on the cutting mat and, using the 45-degree mark, place this on the straight edge of the fabric. And cut! Turn your fabric over, and use the straight side of the ruler to measure the width you need. For 2.5cm (1in) tape you'll need to cut 5cm (2in) of fabric. As you're cutting the strips, your cut line will become longer, so fold the fabric in half, matching up the diagonal edges, and cut through two, three or four layers at a time.

2 To join the strips together, lay two pieces right sides together, overlapping at right angles. Draw a diagonal line from one corner to the other. Pin, then sew across this line. Trim the raw edge back to around 2mm (1⁄8in), then press the seam open.

3 Bias binding involves folding over both of the long edges of the tape into the centre and pressing. The easiest way to do this is to use either a bias binding machine or a small bias tape maker, through which you thread the tape. It folds the strip in two and you press with your iron while pulling the fabric through. If you don't have a tape maker, carefully fold both long edges to the centre of the fabric strips and press. Be careful not to get your fingers too close to the iron!

4a To apply the binding, firstly open up the crease lines and, right sides together, pin across the raw edge of your work. Sew with your machine along the upper crease mark.

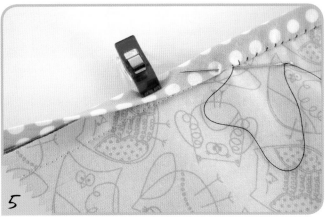

4b If you're applying the bias tape continuously, firstly fold over the end of the tape, open up the creases, pin and machine sew as in step 4a, then overlap the end of the tape by about 5mm (¼in).

5 Now fold the tape over the raw edge, and use a slip stitch to sew by hand. You'll find it easier to use clips to hold the tape in place, and I've used black thread so that you can see the stitches – you'll want to use the same coloured thread as your fabric.

MITRING A CORNER

If the binding is attached around a curve, it will stretch easily, but if you want to mitre a corner, this is how to do it.

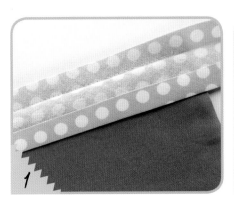

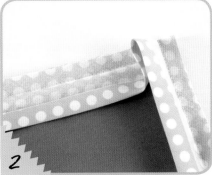

1 Sew along the crease line but stop 5mm (¼in) from the corner and back-tack to stop the stitches from coming undone.

2 Fold the tape along the second side, making a triangular pleat in the corner.

3 Fold the pleat away from your stitch line, and sew straight down the second side. Open up the tape at the corner and you should see a neat mitre forming; as you fold the tape over, mirror the same mitre on the reverse, then slip stitch the other side of the tape in place.

DEBBIE'S TOP TIPS

1 Start with an easy project such as the simple tote with no fastenings, pockets or flaps (see right and pages 30–33). As your skills grow you'll be adding piping, pockets and hardware in no time!

2 Make up your tote in an inexpensive fabric like calico first; that way if things go wrong you're not wasting anything but your time. You may even like your calico version!

3 Always start and stop your stitching with a couple of back-stitches to stop the thread unravelling. Some machines have a lock/fix stitch that puts four stitches on top of each other to do the same job.

4 Read through all the steps for your project before you start sewing. This makes the process easier to follow.

5 Cut your fabric pieces on the grain – this means that the weave of the fabric sits vertically and horizontally. If you cut at an angle (on the bias), your fabric could twist.

6 To help you sew in a straight line with even seam allowances, place a strip of masking tape over the bed of your sewing machine as a guide for your fabric; measure from the needle 5mm (¼in) to the right and place your tape at this point (see right). An elastic band around the free arm works well too.

7 Top-stitching can be a bit daunting, so sew slowly and use a thread that matches your fabric if you're not very confident. Remember, a decorative button is an effective way of hiding wobbly stitches!

8 Pin at right angles to the edge of your fabric. You'll find the layers don't slip, and although you should be taking out your pins as you sew, if the needle accidentally hits a pin, there is less chance of either breaking (see right).

9 Change your sewing machine needle regularly – it is recommended you put a new needle in after every eight hours of sewing. You'll notice a difference to the stitches and even the sound of your machine! It's always good form when you change the needle to take off the needle plate and clear out any lint. Refer to your sewing-machine manual.

10 Relax! Sewing is fun! Don't worry if things go a bit wrong. Put your work down and come back to it the next day – it won't seem half as bad as you thought!

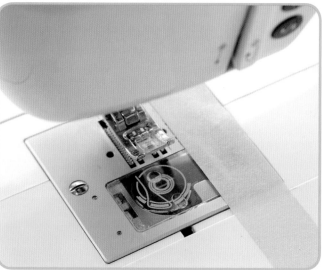

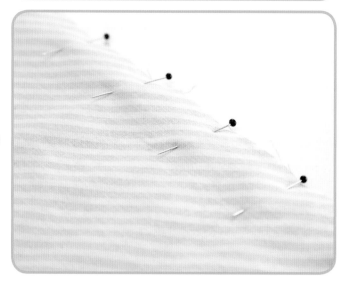

GLOSSARY

Edge stitch:
Stitching close to the edge of your work, for instance around the top of a bag or flap.

Top-stitch:
Stitching on top of your work that can be seen, either decorative or purposeful, for instance around the top of a bag to neaten and hold the lining and outer pieces together.

Raw edge:
The unfinished edge of your fabric.

Right/wrong sides together:
The right side of your fabric is the side you want to be seen; the wrong side is the back of the fabric. When sewing two sections of your bag together, it's usually with two pieces of the same side facing.

Seam allowance:
The distance between your stitches and the edge of the fabric. I've used a 5mm (¼in) seam allowance for the projects in this book.

Back-tack:
Always start and end a row of stitches by sewing a couple of stitches backwards, as this prevents the stitches from coming undone.

Wadding/batting/fleece:
The fleecy layer between the lining and outer sections of the bag, giving it shape and rigidity (see page 13).

Trimmings:
Decorative elements such as the buttons on the quilted bag (see page 70).

Appliqué:
Fabric shapes sewn to the bags as decoration.

The Projects

SEW SIMPLE TOTE

This is the perfect place for a beginner to start: a simple, no-frills bag with no pockets or closures. As your confidence grows you'll soon be adding zips, piping, pockets and flaps to your totes to create your own unique designs! (See also pages 92–93 for advice on customizing your own designs.) For this bag I chose craft cotton for both the outer bag and lining, and gave the bag a bit of sturdiness by backing the outer fabric with fusible fleece.

You will need

- 86.5 x 30.5cm (34 x 12in) outer fabric
- 86.5 x 40.5cm (34 x 16in) fabric for lining
- 86.5 x 30.5cm (34 x 12in) fusible fleece

Finished size

39.5 x 24cm (15½ x 9½in), excluding handles

Using your templates

You will need to use the whole tote outline and the handle outline from TEMPLATE 1. Each of these templates should be placed on the fold of the fabric as indicated.

Template 1

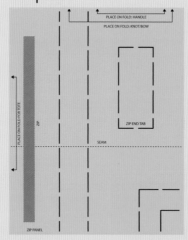

Template 1

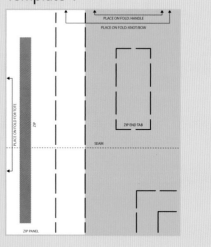

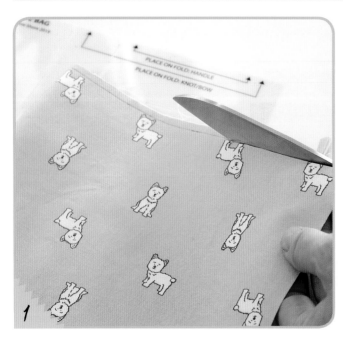

1 Fold your fabric in half, place the template over the fold where indicated, and draw around the tote outline. Repeat to create two pieces of outer fabric the same, two pieces of lining and two pieces of fusible fleece.

To make this bag even simpler, use shop-bought webbing instead of making your own handles.

Tip

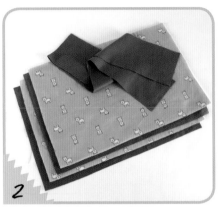

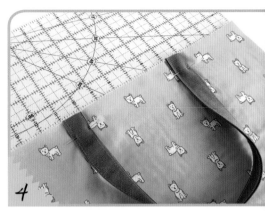

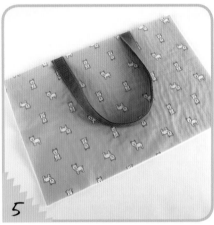

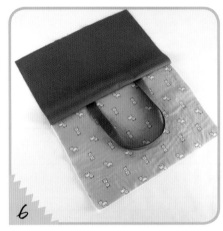

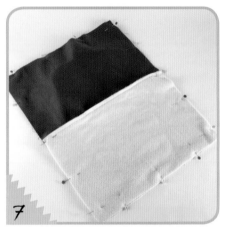

2 Fuse the fleece to the wrong sides of the outer fabric pieces. Draw around the handle template onto the remaining lining fabric, again on the fold as indicated. Cut two handle pieces.

3 Fold the handles in half lengthways and press, then open out, fold the long sides to the centre and press again. Fold in half one last time and press again, then top-stitch along each side. (See also making open-ended handles on page 19.)

4 Along the top edge, measure 10cm (4in) in from each side of the two outer bag pieces, and pin the ends of the handles to these marks, facing inwards, as shown. Make sure they aren't twisted!

5 Tack/baste the handles in place by sewing close to the raw edge.

6 Sew the top of each outer piece to a top of a lining piece, right sides together, sandwiching the handles in between the two pieces.

7 Open out and pin the two fabric pieces together, outer fabric to outer and lining to lining, matching up the seams. Pin across the seam allowance at right angles to the edge of the fabric; doing this makes it easier to remove the pins as you sew, and if by chance you hit a pin with the needle, it will be less likely to break either of them.

8 Sew the two pieces together, but leave a gap of about 10cm (4in) in the bottom lining seam so you can turn it right side out. Don't forget to sew a few stitches backwards at the start and end of your sewing to avoid them snapping when you turn the bag through! Cut across the corners to reduce bulk.

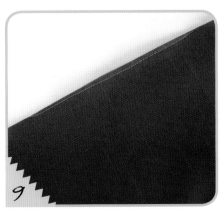

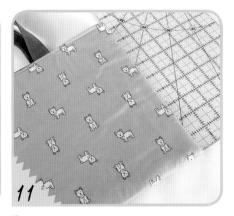

9 Turn the bag right side out. Bring together the two sides of the lining gap with the raw edges tucked inside, and sew straight across on your sewing machine to close. Here, I've used a contrasting coloured thread so you can see where I've sewn; you should use the same colour as your fabric.

10 Push the lining inside the bag and press so that the seam between the outer fabric and lining sits on the top edge. Top-stitch all around the top of the bag, about 5mm (¼in) from the top.

11 That's your very basic tote complete, but if you want to, you can add a bit of interest. Measure and mark along the side seams, 7.5cm (3in) up from the bottom corners.

12 Fold the corners up to the side-seam mark and hand-sew them in place to create a squared-off bag base.

13 Why not add a couple of decorative buttons to hide the join?

CRAFTY ORGANISER

This is such a useful tote to take to craft classes or for storing folders, files and pens – simply add as many pockets as you need! The flap fastens with hook-and-loop tape, with a decorative button to cover the stitches, which makes this design a great alternative for the buttonhole-shy!

An abstract print looks really effective, and also means you don't need to worry about pattern matching at the side seams. My fabric is upholstery weight with a plain cotton lining; I used single-sided fusible foam stabilizer to give a rigid finish. Webbing is a great alternative to making your own handles – if you want to make your own, you'll need to extend the measurements from your template.

You will need

- 76.25 x 91.5cm (30 x 36in) outer fabric
- 43.25 x 56cm (17 x 22in) fabric for lining
- 43.25 x 56cm (17 x 22in) single-sided fusible foam stabilizer
- 17.75 x 28cm (7 x 11in) fusible fleece
- 178cm (70in) of 2.5cm (1in) wide webbing
- 2.5cm (1in) square hook-and-loop fastening

Finished size

39.5 x 24.25cm (15½ x 9½in), excluding handles

34

Using your templates

You will need to use the whole tote outline from TEMPLATE 1, the pocket outline from TEMPLATE 2 and the pointed flap from TEMPLATE 2. The whole tote outline template should be placed on the fold of the fabric as indicated on the template.

Template 1

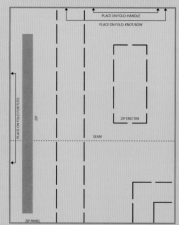

Template 2

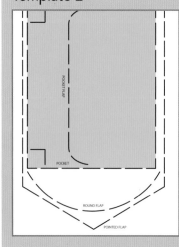

Template 2

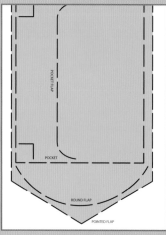

1 Fold your fabric in half and place your tote template over the fold as indicated. Trace the outline onto your fabric.

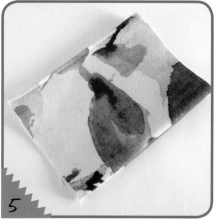

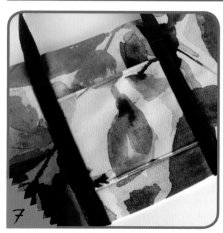

2 Cut out two outer pieces, two lining pieces and two pieces of foam stabilizer. Fuse the foam stabilizer to the wrong sides of the outer fabric pieces.

3 Cut out two pointed flap pieces from outer fabric and one flap piece from fusible fleece. Fuse fleece to the wrong side of one flap piece.

4 Sew the fluffy side of the hook-and-loop fastening to the right side of the un-fleeced flap fabric, 1cm (½in) from the point. Sew the two flap pieces right sides together, leaving the short straight side open. Turn right side out and press, then top-stitch around the seam.

5 Using the template, cut two pocket pieces from outer fabric. Place them right sides together, then sew across the long top and bottom edges to make a tube. Turn right side out and press, then top-stitch along the top seam.

6 Place the pocket onto the back of the bag, centrally, 5cm (2in) up from the bottom. Top-stitch across the base of the pocket.

7 Cut the webbing in half. Pin (or glue) the ends of the handle to the bottom of the bag, 10cm (4in) from either side edge so that they cover the open sides of the pocket. Sew along one side of the handle 20.5cm (8in) from the bottom of the bag, then sew across the handle and down the other side, back to the bottom. Repeat for other end of the handle. Don't sew the handles all the way to the top of the bag.

8 Repeat to attach the handles in the same position on the front of the bag. Sew the second half of the hook-and-loop fastening to the centre, 16.5cm (6½in) down from the top.

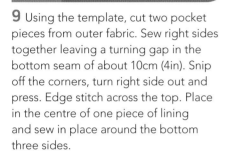

9

10

11

12

13

9 Using the template, cut two pocket pieces from outer fabric. Sew right sides together leaving a turning gap in the bottom seam of about 10cm (4in). Snip off the corners, turn right side out and press. Edge stitch across the top. Place in the centre of one piece of lining and sew in place around the bottom three sides.

10 Hand-sew the button to the right side of the point of the flap. Tack/baste the flap, right sides together, centrally to the top of the back of the bag.

11 Right sides facing, sew the top of the pocketed lining piece to the top of the back of the bag, sandwiching the flap in between the two pieces. Sew the remaining lining piece to the top of the front of the bag, again right sides facing.

12 Sew these two sections right sides together, outer to outer and lining to lining, matching up the seams; leave a turning gap of about 17.75cm (7in) in the bottom of the lining. Snip across the corners.

13 Turn right side out and sew the opening closed.

14 Push the lining inside the bag and press, then top-stitch around the top of the bag to complete.

The back

The front

CURVED FLAP TOTE

A checked print is a cheery print to use and the grid formation makes adding embroidery details easy. I chose a pastel gingham fabric for this tote, but after cutting out the pieces decided it needed a pop of colour, which is why I added the borders of red cross-stitch. The result is quite a 'country' look... I'm imagining picnics in the sunshine, freshly made lemonade and the sound of birds singing! I've backed my fabrics with fusible fleece to add a bit of sturdiness.

Using your templates

You will need to use the whole tote outline with small cut-out corners from TEMPLATE 1, the handle outline from TEMPLATE 1 and the curved flap from TEMPLATE 2. The whole tote outline template and the handle template should be placed on the fold of the fabric as indicated.

Template 1

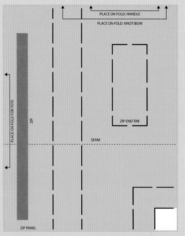

Template 1

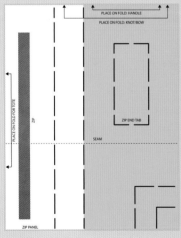

Template 2

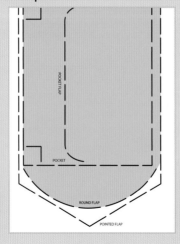

1 Fold your fabric outer and lining pieces in half and place the tote template over the fold as instructed on the template. Draw around the outline, including the smaller cut-out corner.

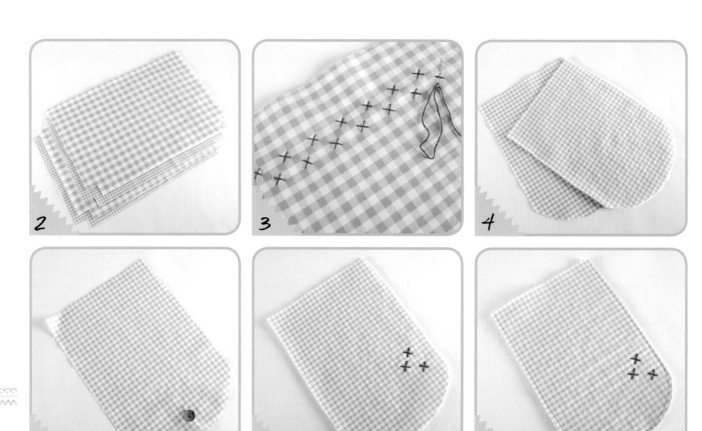

2 Cut out two pieces from outer fabric, two from lining and two from fusible fleece. Fuse fleece to the wrong sides of the outer pieces.

3 Take your embroidery needle and thread and, using the squares woven into the gingham, sew cross stitches in alternate boxes. Embroider as many as you like. See the step 8 photograph for the overall look: I thought two borders were just right for my bag.

4 Cut two curved flap pieces of lining fabric and one of fusible fleece using your template. Fuse fleece to the wrong side of one piece.

5 Fix the slimmer part of the magnetic snap fastener to the centre right side of the non-fleeced flap fabric, 2.5cm (1in) from the edge of the curve.

6 Embroider a few crosses to the right-hand side of the remaining flap piece.

7 Sew the two flap pieces right sides together, leaving the straight top side open. Turn right side out and press, then top-stitch around the seam.

8 Apply the thicker part of the magnetic snap fastener to the centre of the front of the bag, 17.75cm (7in) down from the top.

9 Cut two pieces of handle fabric using the template; adjust the length of the handles if you wish to make them longer or shorter. Make up two closed-ended handles following the instructions on page 19. Sew the ends with a small square of stitches to the top of the front outer bag section, 10cm (4in) from each side and 4cm (1½in) down from the top edge. Don't sew too close to the top edge as you still need to sew in the lining! Add a cross stitch to each end of the handle.

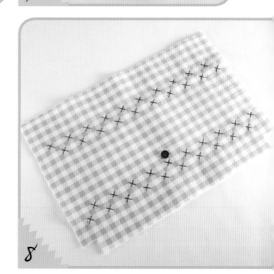

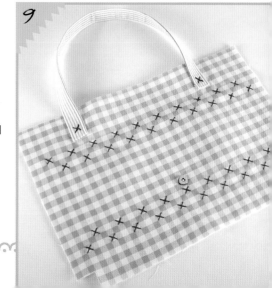

10 Tack/baste the flap, right sides together, to the centre of the back of the bag, then sew the remaining handle on in the same position as on the front of the bag, as shown.

11 Sew the two outer tote sections right sides together, leaving the top and the cut-out corners unsewn.

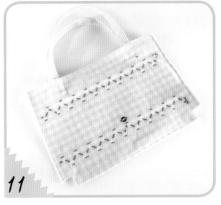

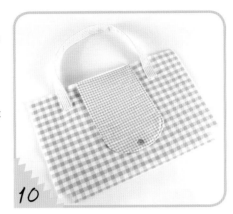

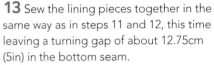

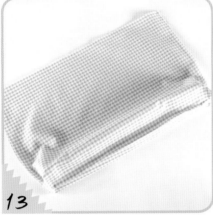

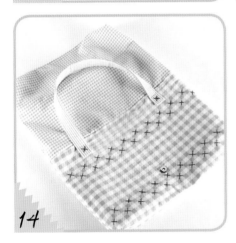

12 Pinch the cut-out corners so that the side seams sit over the bottom seam, and sew straight across.

13 Sew the lining pieces together in the same way as in steps 11 and 12, this time leaving a turning gap of about 12.75cm (5in) in the bottom seam.

14 Turn the outer bag right side out, and drop inside the inside-out lining so that the right sides are together. Sew right around the top edge. Turn right side out and sew the opening closed.

15 Push the lining inside the tote and press, then top-stitch around the top.

TWIST KNOT TOTE

The knotted panel on the front of this tote gives it an edgy, modern twist... quite literally! I've used a zipped panel as a closure to make it a secure bag, so this is the perfect tote for a weekend away. I chose craft-weight cotton for this design, which I've backed with fusible fleece to help it keep its shape.

You will need

- 84 x 28cm (33 x 11in) outer fabric
- 84 x 76.25cm (33 x 30in) plain fabric: I used the same fabric for the lining, bow, zip panel and handles
- 84 x 28cm (33 x 11in) fusible fleece

Finished size

38 x 19 x 9cm (15 x 7½ x 3½in), excluding handles

Using your templates

You will need to use the whole tote outline with large cut-out corners, the knot/bow outline, the handle outline, the zip panel and the zip end tab, all from TEMPLATE 1. The whole tote outline, the bow and the handle templates should be placed on the fold of the fabric as indicated.

Template 1

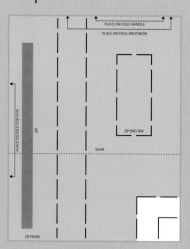

Template 1
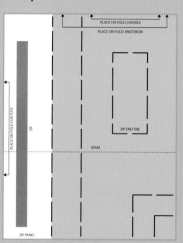

Template 1
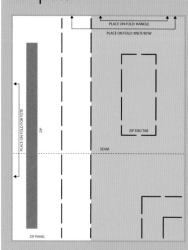

Template 1
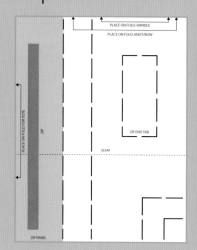

Template 1
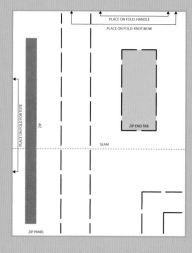

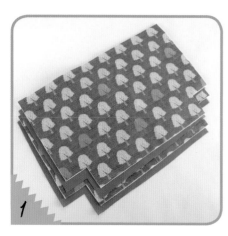

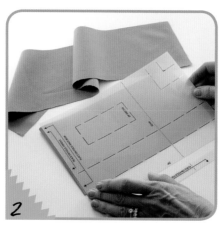

1 Using the tote template with large cut-out corners, fold your fabric in half and cut two pieces from patterned fabric, two from plain and two from fleece. Fuse fleece to the wrong side of the patterned fabric pieces.

2 Place your template over folded plain fabric and cut out two bow pieces.

3 Sew the bow pieces right sides together along the long sides to make a tube, then turn right side out and press.

4 Tie a knot to one side of the bow fabric, then tack/baste it to the sides of the front of the bag, 4cm (1½in) down from the top.

5 Cut two pieces of handle fabric using the template; adjust the length of the handles if you wish to make them longer or shorter. Make up two open-ended handles following the instructions on page 19.

6 Tack/baste the handles, facing downwards, to the top of the front and back pieces of the bag, 9cm (3½in) in from each side.

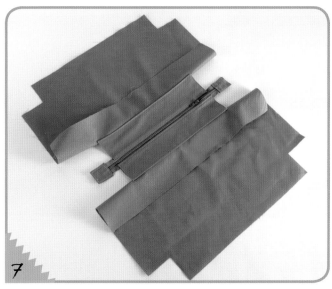

7 Cut out the pieces and make up the zipped panel as explained on pages 16–18. Sew it into the plain lining as instructed.

8 Sew the top of each plain lining piece right sides together to the top of a patterned piece.

9 With the zip open, fold the bag so that the patterned and plain pieces are right sides together. Sew, leaving out the cut-out corners and a turning gap of approximately 12.75cm (5in) in the bottom of the plain lining side.

10 Pinch the cut-out corners so that the side seams sit over the bottom seams, and sew to make the bases squared off. Turn right side out, then sew the opening closed.

11 Push the lining inside the bag and press, then top-stitch around the top edge to complete.

PRETTY PATCHWORK

I used a pre-cut roll of 6.5cm (2½in) strips of patterned quilting cotton for this pretty, summery tote, then picked out the red colour from the flowers for the base and handles.

You will need

- Five strips of 6.5cm (2½in) wide fabric in coordinating colours measuring 76.25cm (30in) each (pre-cut strips are usually 112cm/44in in length)
- 84 x 61cm (33 x 24in) plain fabric: I used the same red fabric for the base, handles and lining
- 84 x 51cm (33 x 20in) fusible fleece
- 10cm (4in) hair elastic
- Button

Finished size

38 x 19 x 9cm (15 x 7½ x 3½in), excluding handles

Using your templates

You will need to use the whole tote outline with large cut-out corners and the handle outline from TEMPLATE 1. Each of these templates should be placed on the fold of the fabric as indicated.

Template 1

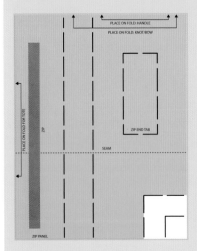

Template 1

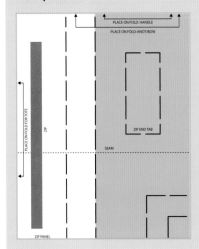

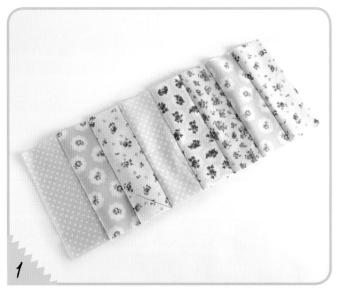

1 Cut your strips of fabric into 20.5cm (8in) lengths. Sew the strips right sides together until you have joined eight in a row. Repeat to create a second panel. Press the seams to one side; if you have light and dark fabrics, press the seams towards the dark side.

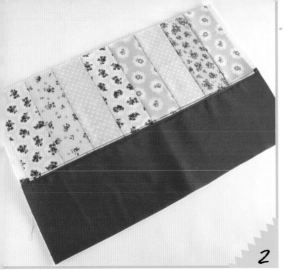

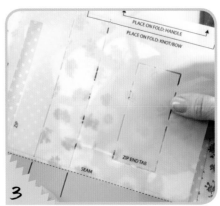

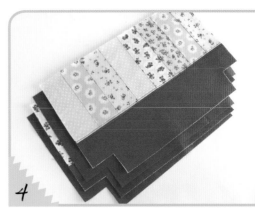

2

3

4

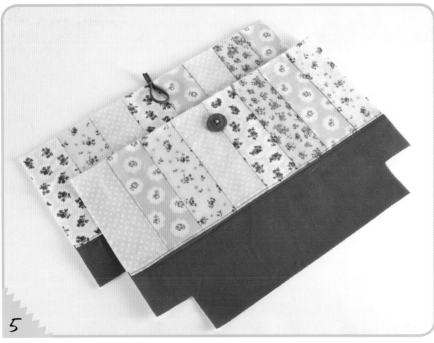

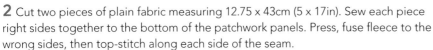

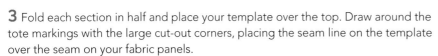

5

6

7

2 Cut two pieces of plain fabric measuring 12.75 x 43cm (5 x 17in). Sew each piece right sides together to the bottom of the patchwork panels. Press, fuse fleece to the wrong sides, then top-stitch along each side of the seam.

3 Fold each section in half and place your template over the top. Draw around the tote markings with the large cut-out corners, placing the seam line on the template over the seam on your fabric panels.

4 Cut each patchwork outer bag piece to shape, then cut two pieces from lining fabric as well.

5 Sew the hair elastic in half, facing downwards, to the centre top of one of the panels (this is now your back panel). Sew the button to the opposite (front) side, 4cm (1½in) down from the centre top.

6 Cut two pieces of handle fabric using the template; adjust the length of the handles if you wish to make them longer or shorter. Make up two open-ended handles following the instructions on page 19; I've used fusible fleece in the handles to give them firmness.

7 Tack/baste the handles, facing downwards, to the top of each side of the tote, 10cm (4in) in from either side.

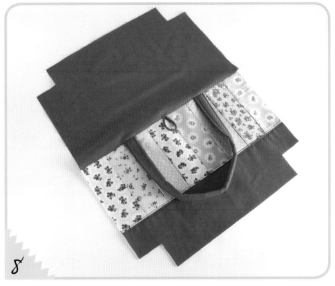

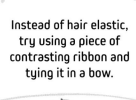

8 Sew the top of each outer piece right sides together to the top of a lining piece.

9 Pin both sections right sides together, outer to outer and lining to lining, matching up the seams. Sew all the way round the edge, leaving out the cut-out corners unsewn and a turning gap of about 12.75cm (5in) in the bottom of the lining.

10 Pinch the cut-out corners together so that the side seams sit over the bottom seams, and sew to make the bases squared off.

11 Pull the tote the right way out through the turning gap, then sew the opening closed.

12 Push the lining inside the bag and press, then top-stitch around the top edge to complete.

Instead of hair elastic, try using a piece of contrasting ribbon and tying it in a bow.

Tip

PERFECTLY PIPED

The contrast base of this tote, edged with piping, adds a sophisticated finishing touch; use laminated fabric for the base to make it practical and wipe-clean. The striped fabric I've used is upholstery fabric, the base and lining are linen, and I've backed the outer fabric pieces with fusible fleece to make the bag sturdy. This tote closes with a simple magnetic snap fastener.

You will need

- 61 x 53.5cm (24 x 21in) striped fabric
- 41 x 41cm (16 x 16in) plain fabric
- 41 x 25.5cm (16 x 10in) fusible fleece
- 81.5cm (32in) of 5mm (¼in) wide piping cord
- 81.5cm (32in) of 2.5cm (1in) wide tape for the piping: I used a strip of my striped fabric
- Magnetic snap fastener

Finished size
38 x 19 x 9cm (15 x 7½ x 3½in), excluding handles

Using your templates

You will need to use the whole tote outline with large cut-out corners and the handle outline from TEMPLATE 1. Each of these templates should be placed on the fold of the fabric as indicated.

Template 1

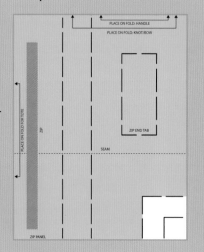

Template 1

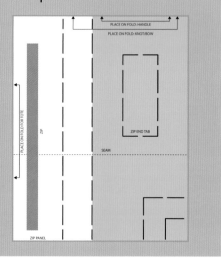

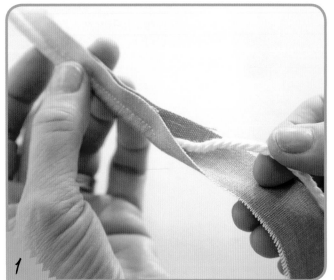

1 Wrap the strips of fabric around the piping cord and sew with the zipper foot on your sewing machine. Cut in half.

Make your piping stand out by using a bold, contrasting coloured fabric.

Tip

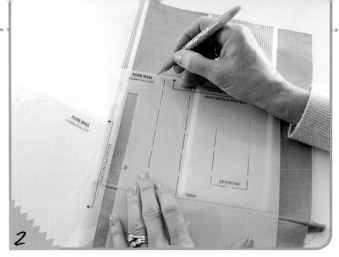

2 Cut two pieces of striped fabric measuring 41 x 17.75cm (16 x 7in) and two plain pieces measuring 41 x 12.75cm (16 x 5in). Sew each striped fabric piece to a plain piece, right sides facing, sandwiching the piping between and aligning the raw edges. Press.

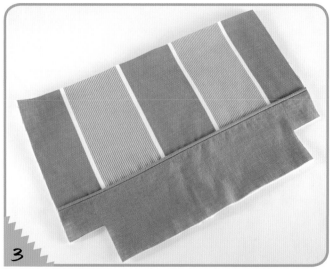

3 Fold your piped fabric in half and place your template over the fold as indicated, with the seam line across the piping. Using the largest sized cut-out corners, cut out the fabric. Repeat for the other side of the bag. Fuse fleece to the wrong side of each fabric piece. Pull the cord from the piping carefully and trim 5mm (¼in) from each end. This will help when sewing the side seams. Cut out two lining pieces from the same template.

4 Cut two pieces of handle fabric using the template; adjust the length of the handles if you wish to make them longer or shorter. Make up two open-ended handles, as on page 19. Tack/baste these facing downwards to the top of each side of the bag, 11.5cm (4½in) in from each side.

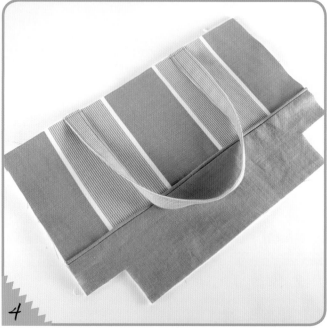

5 Pin the two sections right sides together, and sew along the sides and base, leaving the cut-out corners unsewn. Remove the pins. Pinch the cut-out corners so that the side seams sit over the bottom seam, and sew.

6 Turn right side out.

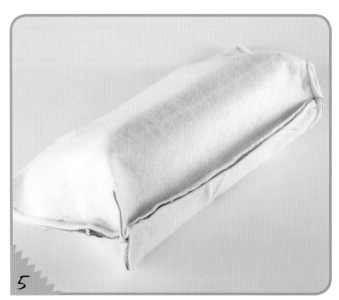

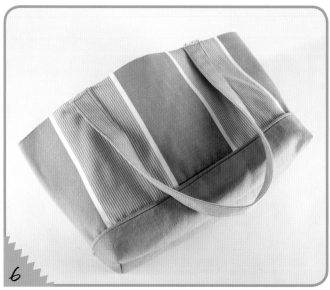

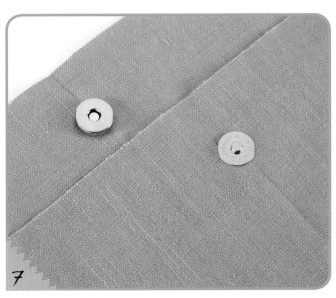

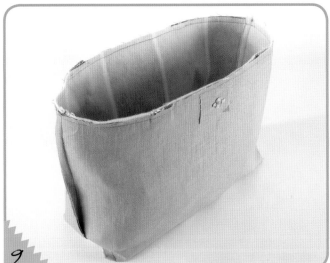

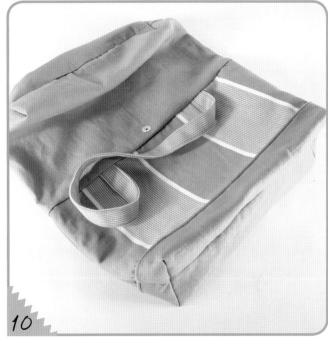

7 Fit one part of the magnetic snap fastener to the centre of each lining piece, 2.5cm (1in) down from the top.

8 Sew the two lining pieces right sides together in the same way as the outer fabric, leaving the cut-out corners unsewn, but this time leave a turning gap in the base of about 10cm (4in).

9 Drop the outer bag inside the lining with right sides together, then sew right the way around the top.

10 Turn right side out, then sew the turning gap closed.

11 Push the lining inside the bag and press, then top-stitch around the top edge to complete your lovely bag.

PATCH POCKET TOTE

The pocket on the front of this tote is a handy place to keep your essentials to hand, and I've secured it with a magnetic snap fastener. The zipped panel in the lining also adds extra security. My patterned fabric is upholstery fabric and the black lining is linen-look cotton. I backed the outer panels with fusible fleece.

Using your templates

You will need to use the whole tote outline with small cut-out corners, the handle outline, the zip panel and the zip end tab all from TEMPLATE 1. You will also need the pocket and pocket flap templates from TEMPLATE 2. The whole tote outline template and the handle template should be placed on the fold of the fabric as indicated.

Template 1
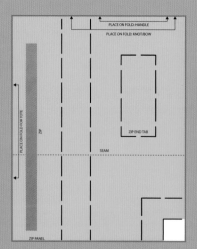

Template 1
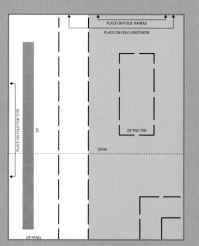

Template 1
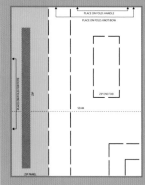

Template 1
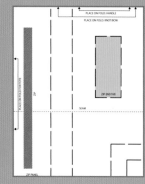

Template 2
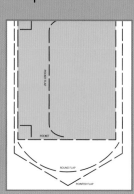

Template 2
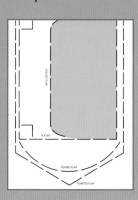

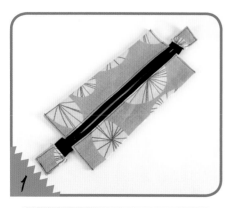

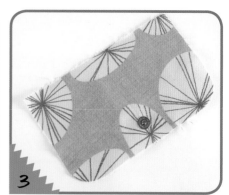

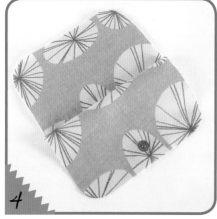

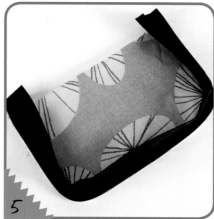

1 Make up a zipped panel as on pages 16–18.

2 Fold your patterned and plain fabrics in half and place the tote template over the fold as indicated. Draw around the outline, including the smaller cut-out corners. Cut out two patterned pieces, two plain pieces and two pieces of fusible fleece. Fuse fleece to the wrong sides of the patterned pieces.

3 Using the template, cut out two pocket flaps and two pocket pieces. Fuse fleece to the wrong side of one of each. Fit the slimmer part of the magnetic snap fastener to the centre of the unfleeced flap piece, 2.5cm (1in) up from the edge of the curved side.

4 Sew the two flap pieces right sides together across the straight top edge.

5 Fold so that the wrong sides are facing and press. Apply bias binding around the curved edge, with 1cm (½in) of tape extending at each end (see pages 24–25).

6 Fold the tape over the edge and tuck the ends inwards to make neat, then hand-sew with slip stitch.

7 Fix the second half of the magnetic snap fastener to the padded front of the pocket, 6.5cm (2½in) from the top. Sew the two pocket pieces right sides together across the top as shown.

8 Fold so that the wrong sides are together and press. Edge stitch along the top seam. Apply bias tape around the three raw edges, mitring the corners as you sew.

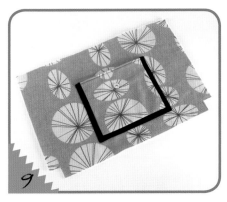

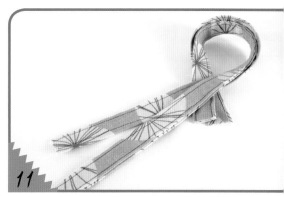

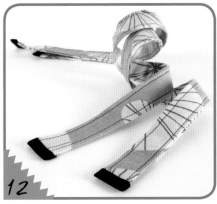

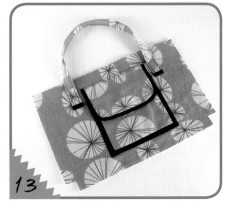

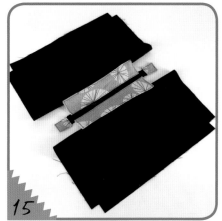

9 Pin the pocket to the centre of the front bag panel, 4cm (1½in) up from the bottom. Sew around the bottom three sides, then remove the pins.

10 Place the flap over the top so that the magnetic snap fastens, then sew across the top of the flap to secure it to the bag.

11 Cut two pieces of handle fabric using the template; adjust the length of the handles if you wish to make them longer or shorter. Make up two open-ended handles, as explained on page 19.

12 Add bias binding to each end, folding in the edges of the tape to make the ends neat as shown.

13 Sew one handle to the front of the bag either side of the pocket, 7.5cm (3in) from the top and sides of the bag, in a box shape to make the join strong.

14 Sew the second handle to the back bag panel in the same position. Pin the two bag pieces right sides together and sew, leaving the top and cut-out corners open. Pinch the cut-out corners so that the side seams sit over the bottom seam and sew; turn right side out.

15 Insert the zipped panel into the lining (see page 19).

16 Sew the sides and bottom of the lining pieces together, right sides facing, leaving a turning gap in the bottom seam of about 12.75cm (5in). Sew the cut-out corners to make the base squared off. Drop the lining inside the bag, wrong sides facing, and tack/baste together around the top.

17 Apply bias binding around the top. I prefer the join of my binding to sit over a seam so it's not too noticeable. Machine sew to the outside of the bag, fold over and hand-sew to the lining.

PURSE WITH FLAP

If you have some stash fabric lying about, why not sew yourself a purse? The patterned fabric is quilting cotton and I've used linen for the lining. Fusible fleece gives the purse form. I added a decorative button to the flap to give it more of a 'designer' look. The ribbon wristlet means I can be hands-free!

You will need

- 35.5 x 28cm (14 x 11in) patterned fabric
- 35.5 x 28cm (14 x 11in) fabric for the lining
- 35.5 x 28cm (14 x 11in) fusible fleece
- Magnetic snap fastener
- 30.5cm (12in) of 1cm (½in) wide ribbon
- Decorative button (optional)

Finished size

16.5 x 14 x 3.75cm (6½ x 5½ x 1½in), excluding handles

58

Using your template

You will need to use the pocket outline and the pocket flap outline from TEMPLATE 2.

Template 2

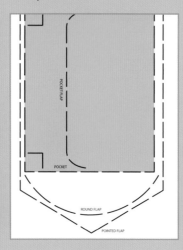

Template 2

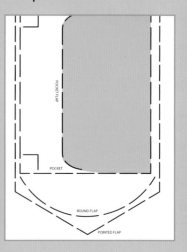

1 Draw around the tote pocket onto the back of your fabric, as shown. Before cutting, place the flap template over the top of the pocket shape and draw around this template to extend your pattern.

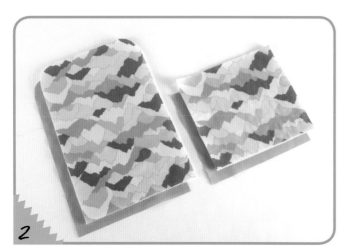

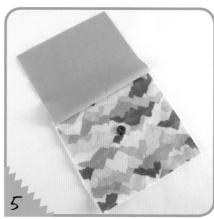

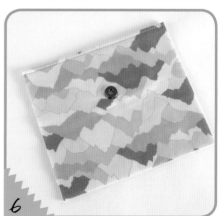

2 Cut one patterned and one lining piece from this elongated pocket shape. Draw around the pocket template again and cut one patterned and one lining piece. Fuse fleece to the wrong sides of the patterned pieces.

3 Apply the thicker part of the magnetic snap fastener to the small patterned piece, centrally, 6.5cm (2½in) down from the top. Fit the remaining part of the snap to the large lining piece, centrally, 2.5cm (1in) from the edge of the curved side. (See page 23 for further instruction.)

4 Loop the ribbon in half and tack/baste to one side of the large patterned piece, facing inwards, 12.75cm (5in) from the bottom.

5 Sew the top of the small lining piece right sides together to the top of the small patterned piece.

6 Fold over so that the wrong sides are facing, then press. Top-stitch across the top edge.

Add a ribbon with a small D-ring on the end to the inside seam to keep your house keys handy.

Tip

7 Place this section right sides together with the large patterned piece and sew straight across the bottom.

8 Place the remaining lining piece right sides together over the top, with the small section sandwiched in the centre. Sew all the way around, leaving a turning gap in the bottom of about 7.5cm (3in). Snip off the corners and cut around the curve with pinking shears.

9 Turn right side out and hand-sew the opening closed.

10 Flip over the pocket and press. Top-stitch around the flap.

11 Add the button to the flap and you're finished!

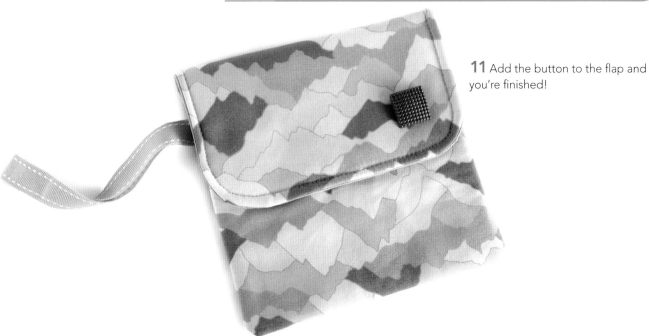

PURSE WITH ZIP

This small zipped purse is the perfect size for cosmetics, loose change or even a sewing repair kit, and would make a well-received gift for the modern girl. My fabric is craft-weight cotton, stiffened with fusible fleece. I like to use zips that are too long for my projects and cut them down to size – that way I can keep the slider out of the way when I'm sewing! I've kept this purse plain and simple, but you could easily add a wristlet, appliqué, buttons or bows to decorate as you like.

You will need

- 41 x 18cm (16 x 7in) outer fabric
- 41 x 18cm (16 x 7in) fabric for lining
- 41 x 18cm (16 x 7in) fusible fleece
- 20.5cm (8in) zip
- 12.75cm (5in) of 5mm (¼in) wide ribbon

Finished size

18 x 12.75 x 4cm (7 x 5 x 1½in)

If you want to add a bit of colour to your fabric, use fabric dye pens to colour in the print, then iron them to set the ink.

Tip

Using your template

You will need to use the pocket outline with cut-out corners from TEMPLATE 2.

Template 2

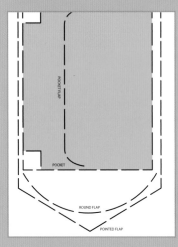

POCKET FLAP

POCKET

ROUND FLAP

POINTED FLAP

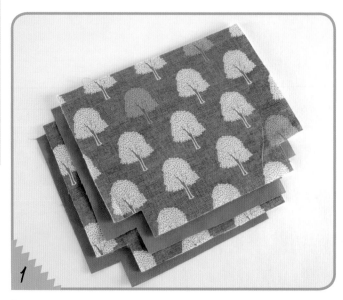

1 Cut two outer and two lining pieces from the pocket template, with the cut-out corners at the bottom. Fuse fleece to the wrong side of the outer pieces.

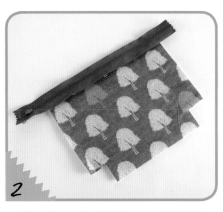

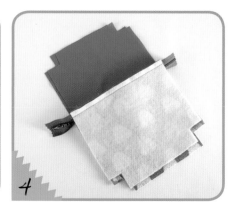

2 With the slider out of the way, sew the top of one outer piece to the zip tape, right sides together; you may find it easier to hand-sew the open end of the zip closed first.

3 Sew a lining piece to the opposite side, sandwiching the zip in between the two pieces as shown.

4 Repeat with the outer and lining pieces on the opposite side of the zip tape.

5 Open the zip, then sew the two sides right sides together, outer to outer and lining to lining, leaving the cut-out corners unsewn and with a turning gap in the bottom seam of the lining of about 10cm (4in). When you approach the zip, tuck it towards the lining side.

6 Pinch the cut-out corners so that the side seams sit over the base seam, and sew straight across to make the base of the bag squared off.

7 Trim off the ends of the zip, then turn the purse right side out. Sew the opening closed.

8 Push the lining inside the purse and press. Fold the ribbon in half, thread through the end of the zip tab and knot.

FOLDAWAY SHOPPER

Keep this folded tote inside your handbag for those occasions when you need an extra bag for your shopping. The tote is unlined to make it easy to fold into the pocket, so to keep the seams neat I've used a French seam which encloses the raw edges.

You will need

- 43 x 56cm (17 x 22in) plain fabric
- 56 x 41cm (22 x 16in) patterned fabric
- 51cm (20in) of 5mm (¼in) wide ribbon
- 4 buttons

Finished size

39.5 x 24cm (15½ x 9½in); when folded, 16.5 x 14cm (6½ x 5½in)

Using your templates

You will need to use the whole tote outline and the handle outline from TEMPLATE 1 as well as the pocket outline from TEMPLATE 2. The whole tote outline template and the handle template should be placed on the fold of the fabric as indicated.

Template 1

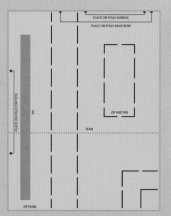

Template 1

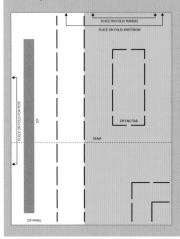

Template 2

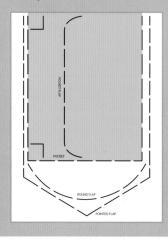

French seams can be used in unlined clothing or with sheer fabrics – a useful technique to learn.

Tip

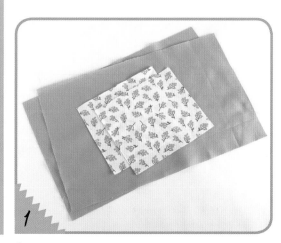

1 Using your tote template, cut two bag pieces from plain fabric. Cut two pocket pieces from patterned fabric.

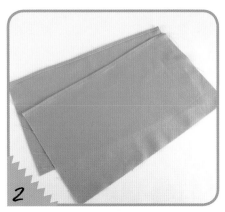

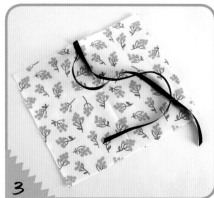

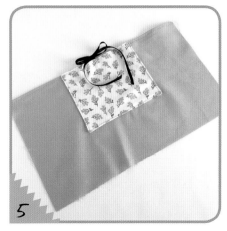

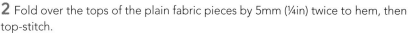

2 Fold over the tops of the plain fabric pieces by 5mm (¼in) twice to hem, then top-stitch.

3 Fold the ribbon in half, then tack/baste to the right side centre top of one of the pocket pieces of fabric.

4 Making sure the ribbon ends are tucked out of the way, sew the two pocket pieces right sides together, leaving a turning gap in the bottom seam of about 7.5cm (3in). Turn right side out and press. Edge stitch across the top.

5 Pin the pocket to the centre top of one of the plain pieces of fabric, then sew around the bottom three sides. Remove the pins.

6 Cut two pieces of handle fabric using the template; adjust the length of the handles if you wish to make them longer or shorter. Make up two closed-end handles following the instructions on page 19.

7 Place the handles at an angle, either side of the pocket. Sew a box shape to secure, then add the buttons on top.

8 Sew the second handle to the other side of the bag in the same position as the first, as shown.

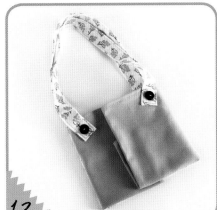

9 Pin the two plain pieces *wrong* sides together and sew around the sides and bottom edge, leaving the top open. Trim the seams back to 3mm (⅛in).

10 Turn inside out, and re-sew over the seams, trapping the raw edges inside.

11 Turn back to the right side.

12 Flip the bag over so the pocket is facing downwards. Fold the bottom of the bag upwards and both sides of the bag inwards over the pocket.

13 Turn the pocket inside out with the bag inside, then tuck in the handles.

14 Tie the ribbon around the pocket.

QUILTED TOTE WITH BUTTON TRIM

This a great project for using up mismatched buttons. I managed to put together a whole collection of grey, but this tote would look fun if you used multicoloured buttons instead! I've also made the handles shorter by cutting them down to 41cm (16in), and edged them with contrasting coloured bias tape. The fabric is craft cotton, and to make the stitches sink into the fabric when quilting I've used two layers of wool wadding/batting. If you want to add a closure to this bag, I'd suggest the zipped panel or magnetic snap fastener in the lining, so as not to cover up the button detail.

You will need

- 84 x 38cm (33 x 15in) outer fabric
- 84 x 28cm (33 x 11in) fabric for lining
- 84 x 56cm (33 x 22in) wadding/batting
- 165cm (65in) of 1cm (½in) wide bias binding
- 36 buttons
- Repositionable spray fabric adhesive
- Ruler and erasable marking pen

Finished size

38 x 19 x 9cm (15 x 7½ x 3½in), excluding handles

Using your templates

You will need to use the whole tote outline with large cut-out corners and the handle outline from TEMPLATE 1. Both will need to be placed on the fold of the fabric as indicated on the template.

Template 1

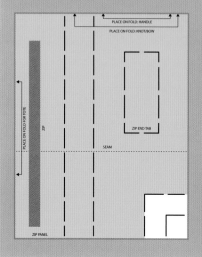

Template 1

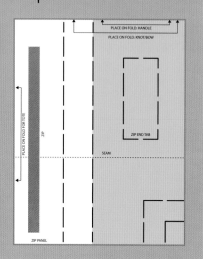

1 Fold your fabric in half and place the template over the fold as indicated on the template. Cut out two outer and two lining pieces, and cut out the largest-sized corners. Fuse two layers of wadding/batting to the wrong side of the outer fabric pieces.

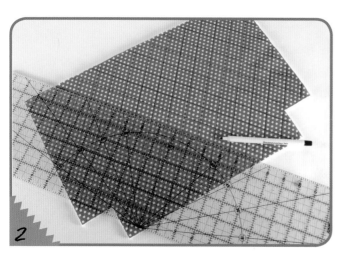

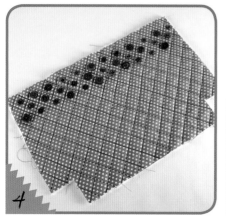

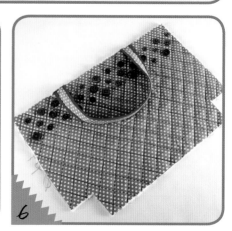

2 Draw 45-degree lines, 2.5cm (1in) apart, across the outer fabric to form a grid, using your ruler and erasable marking pen.

3 Sew over the lines with a straight stitch; I used a contrasting thread to make a feature of my quilting. Use a walking foot for your sewing machine if you have one, as this will help to feed the layers evenly.

4 Sew three rows of buttons, positioned in the centre of each box, to the top of the fabric. Be careful to keep the buttons away from your seam allowance though – we don't want any broken sewing-machine needles!

5 Make up two open-ended handles following the instructions on page 19. Fold the bias tape in half lengthways and press. Wrap this around the long sides of the handles and top-stitch in place.

6 Tack/baste the handles, facing inwards, to the top of the outer bag pieces, 10cm (4in) in from each side.

I've just added buttons to the front of the bag; be careful if you sew them to the back as they may catch on your clothing!

Tip

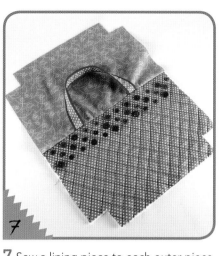

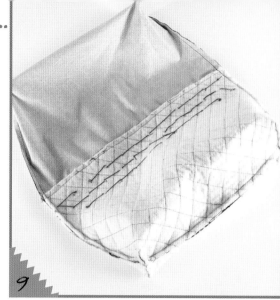

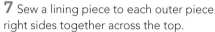

7 Sew a lining piece to each outer piece right sides together across the top.

8 Sew the two sections right sides together, leaving the cut-out corners unsewn and with a turning gap of about 12.75cm (5in) in the base of the lining.

9 Pinch the cut-out corners so that the side seams sit over the bottom seams and sew straight across to make the bag base squared off.

10 Turn right side out, then sew the opening closed.

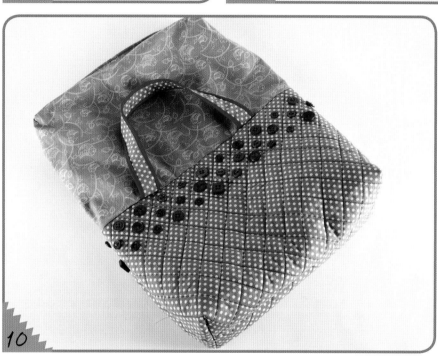

11 Push the lining inside the bag and top-stitch around the top edge. You may find it helpful to use the zipper foot on your sewing machine to avoid hitting the buttons!

BEACH BAG

I used the curved flap template to make a pocket for sunglasses on my beach bag, which can be filled with sun creams, reading matter and loose change for ice cream! I've used craft cotton in a summery print, but consider using laminated fabric for the lining if you'll need to carry wet swimming costumes around.

You will need

- 102 x 30.5cm (40 x 12in) outer fabric
- 102 x 30.5cm (40 x 12in) fabric for lining
- 102 x 30.5cm (40 x 12in) fusible fleece
- 168cm (66in) of 2.5cm (1in) wide webbing
- 3 decorative buttons

Finished size

39.5 x 21.5 x 4cm (15½ x 8½ x 1½in), excluding handles

Using your templates

You will need to use the whole tote outline with small cut-out corners from TEMPLATE 1 and the round flap outline from TEMPLATE 2. The whole tote outline template will need to be placed on the fold of the fabric, as indicated.

Template 1

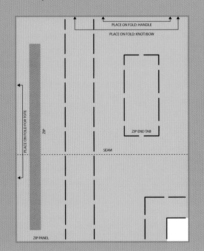

Template 2

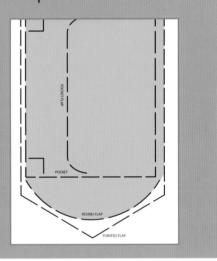

1 Fold your fabric in half and draw around the tote outline with the small cut-out corners. You'll need two from outer fabric, and two from lining. Fuse fleece to the wrong sides of the outer pieces.

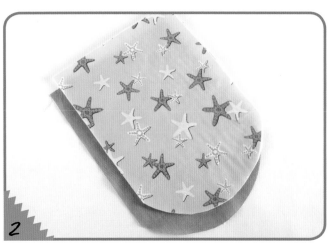

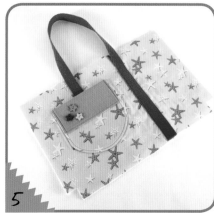

2 Use the curved flap template to cut out one outer and one lining fabric piece. Fuse fleece to the wrong side of the outer fabric.

3 Sew the flap pieces right sides together, leaving a 5cm (2in) gap in one straight side for turning. Snip across the corners, and trim the curved seam with pinking shears.

4 Turn right side out and press. Edge stitch across the straight side, then fold over the top of the flap so the lining shows by 7.5cm (3in). Hand-sew the buttons to one side. Now you have your pocket!

5 Cut a 71cm (28in) length of webbing. Pin to one outer piece of bag fabric, 12.75cm (5in) from each side, starting with one end of the handle at the bottom, and the other end 15.25cm (6in) from the bottom. Sew along both sides of the handle to fix to the bag, but stop sewing 5cm (2in) from the top of the bag. Remove the pins. Pin the pocket over the shorter end of the handle and sew in place. Remove the pins.

6 Sew the remaining webbing handle to the back of the bag, with the ends of the handle at the bottom, ensuring that the handles are the same length on both bag pieces; position the handles 12.75cm (5in) from each side. Again, stop sewing 5cm (2in) from the top.

If you're making holiday bags for the whole family, it would be fun to add their initials to the pockets to make each one personal!

Tip

7 Sew the two outer bag sections right sides together, leaving the top edge and cut-out corners unsewn. Pinch the cut-out corners so that the side seams sit on top of the base seam, and sew straight across to make the bottom of the bag squared off.

8 Turn right side out. Sew together the lining pieces right sides facing along the sides and base, leaving the cut-out corners unsewn, this time leaving a turning gap of about 20.5cm (8in) in the base seam. Drop the outer bag inside the lining with right sides together and sew around the top.

9 Turn right side out and sew the opening closed.

10 Push the lining inside the bag, then top-stitch around the top edge. Anyone for ice cream?

DRAWSTRING BAG

This pretty pouch can be filled with toiletries, making it an ideal gift, or it could be useful storage for lingerie and nightwear. Add a personal touch with appliquéd initials or try quilting the fabric to create a luxurious feel.

Make up the bag in mesh fabric without a lining, using the French-seam technique to make a perfect storage pouch for bathroom items!

Tip

You will need

- 61 x 43cm (24 x 17in) outer fabric
- 61 x 53.5cm (24 x 21in) fabric for lining
- 61 x 43cm (24 x 17in) fusible fleece
- 122cm (48in) of 1cm (½in) wide ribbon
- Bodkin or safety pin

Finished size

20.5 x 33 x 5cm (8 x 13 x 2in)

Using your template

You will need to use the whole tote outline with small cut-out corners from TEMPLATE 1. You will not need to place the template on the fold of the fabric this time.

Template 1

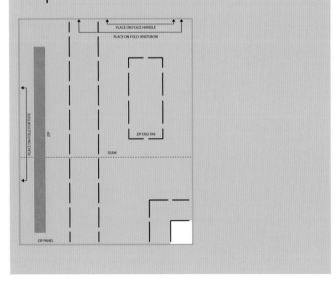

1 This time we're not going to use the template on the fold of fabric, so place it on a single layer of fabric and draw around the tote outline. Draw the small cut-out corner, then flip the template over and draw the small cut-out corner on the opposite bottom side.

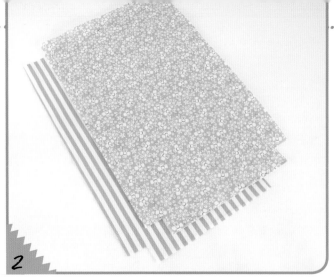

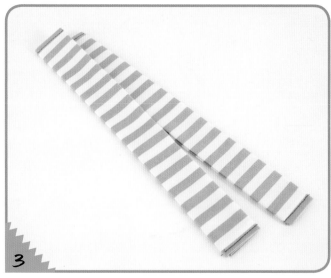

2 Cut out two outer pieces of fabric from this shape, and two lining pieces. Fuse the fleece to the wrong side of the outer pieces.

3 Cut two strips of lining fabric measuring 25.5 x 10cm (10 x 4in). Fold the short ends over by 1cm (½in) and press, then fold the strips in half lengthways wrong sides together and press. Unfold, then fold the long sides to the centre, fold in half again and press. You will have two strips now measuring 23.5 x 2.5cm (9 x 1in). Sew across the short ends.

4 Pin, then sew one strip to the right side of each outer piece, centrally, 7.5cm (3in) from the top. Sew along each long side, leaving the short ends open to form a channel for the ribbon. Remove your pins.

5 Sew the top of a striped lining piece to the top of each outer piece, right sides together.

6 Pin the two halves of the bag right sides together, outer to outer and lining to lining, matching up the seams. Sew all around, apart from the cut-out corners, and leave a turning gap in the bottom of the lining of about 10cm (4in). Pinch the cut-out corners so that the side seams sit over the base seams, and sew straight across to make the bag base squared off.

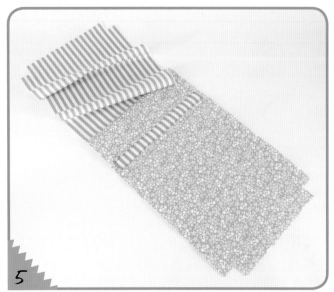

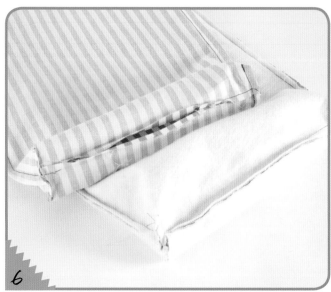

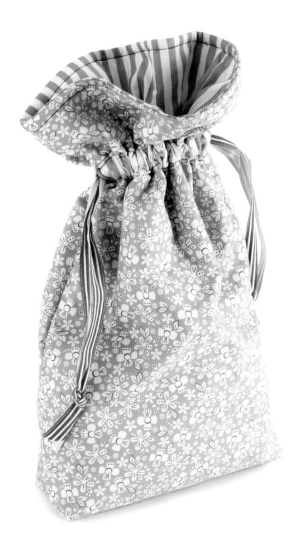

7 Turn right side out and sew the opening closed.

8 Push the lining inside the bag and press. Edge stitch around the top edge.

9 Cut the ribbon in half. Using either a bodkin or safety pin, thread the ribbon through one channel, then back through the other. Knot the ends together. Repeat with the second ribbon but thread in the opposite direction this time so the ribbon emerges from the other side of the bag.

10 Pull both ribbons to close the bag.

DOUBLE POCKET OFFICE TOTE

Two large pockets make it easy to organize the contents of your bag. This clever and practical style of tote will leave your friends wondering how you made it!

You will need

- 84 x 61cm (33 x 24in) outer fabric
- 107 x 76.25cm (42 x 30in) fabric for lining
- 56 x 71cm (22 x 28in) fusible fleece
- 1 button

Finished size

39.5 x 24 x 2cm (15½ x 9½ x ¾in), excluding handles

Using your templates

You will need to use the whole tote outline from TEMPLATE 1, the handle outline from TEMPLATE 1 and the curved flap outline from TEMPLATE 2. The whole tote outline template and the handle template should be placed on the fold of the fabric as indicated.

Template 1

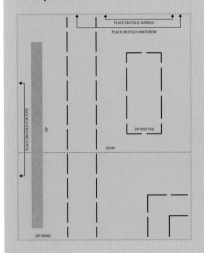

Template 1

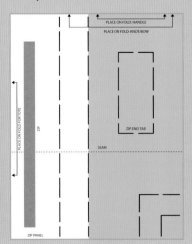

Template 2

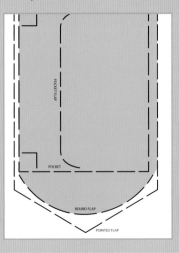

1 Use your template to cut out four outer fabric tote pieces and four lining pieces, without cutting out the corners. Fuse fleece to the wrong sides of the outer pieces. Cut two curved flaps from lining fabric, then fuse fleece to the wrong side of one flap piece.

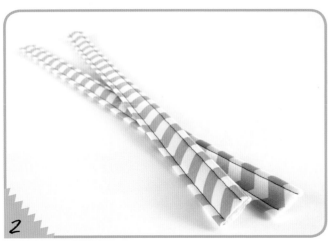

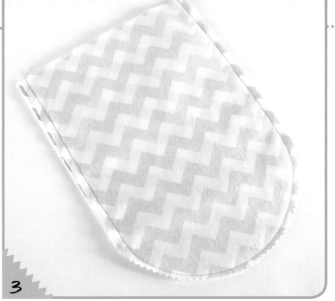

2

3

4

5

6

2 Cut two pieces of handle fabric using the template; adjust the length of the handles if you wish to make them longer or shorter. Fuse fleece to the wrong sides and make up the open-ended handles following the instructions on page 19.

3 Sew the two flap pieces right sides together, leaving the straight top end open. Snip around the curves with pinking shears.

4 Turn the flap right side out, fold the open end inwards by 1cm (½in) and press. Top-stitch around the curved seam.

5 Sew the buttonhole centrally, 2.5cm (1in) from the curved edge. I always sew a practice buttonhole first so that I can make sure the size and position are correct.

6 Sew the flap right sides together to the centre of one of the outer fabric pieces in a box shape, 5.75cm (2¼in) from the top. This will be the back of the bag. Set this piece aside until step 12.

Add another pocket to make this into a triple-pocket bag!

Tip

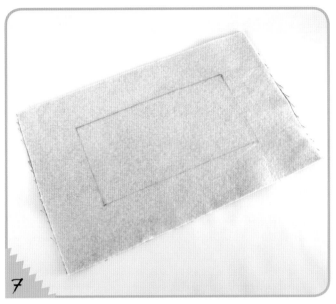

7 Take one of the outer fabric pieces, and draw a rectangular box in the centre of the back, measuring 25.5 x 12.75cm (10 x 5in).

8 Pin this piece right sides together with a second outer piece and sew around the box. Remove the pins.

9 Fold all four edges of one side of the fabric to the centre and secure with clips (or pins if you don't have clips).

10 Place another outer fabric piece right sides together down on top, with the folded layer in the centre, and sew around the bottom three sides.

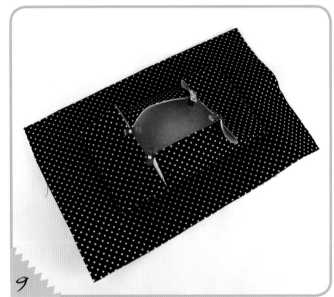

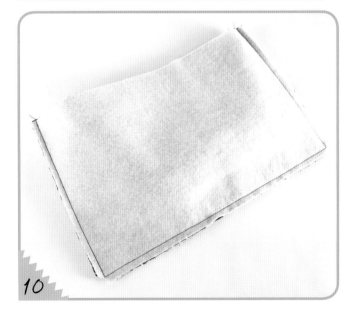

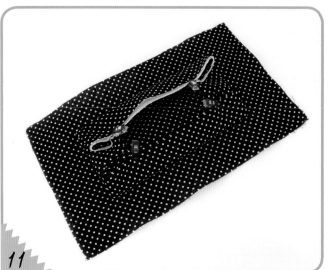

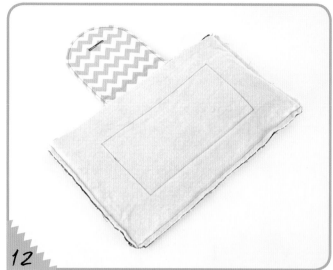

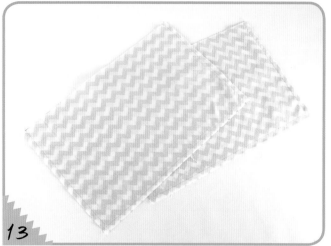

11 Turn right side out. Fold the pocket into the centre and clip or pin it out of the way as before.

12 Place this piece and the back panel of the bag right sides together with the pocket sandwiched in the middle, and sew around the bottom three sides. Turn right side out.

13 Take the four lining pieces and sew right sides together in pairs, leaving the top edges open. Turn the top edges of each lining pocket over by 5mm (¼in) and press, then snip across the corners. Repeat to turn under and press 5mm (¼in) around the top edges of the outer bag.

14 Drop one lining piece inside one of the bag sections with the wrong sides together and pin around the top. Take one of the handles, push each end in between the lining and outer fabric on the front of the bag, 7.5cm (3in) from each side and pin.

15 Repeat with the remaining pocket and lining, pinning the handles on the same side as the flap.

16 Carefully sew around the top of each pocket and remove the pins.

16

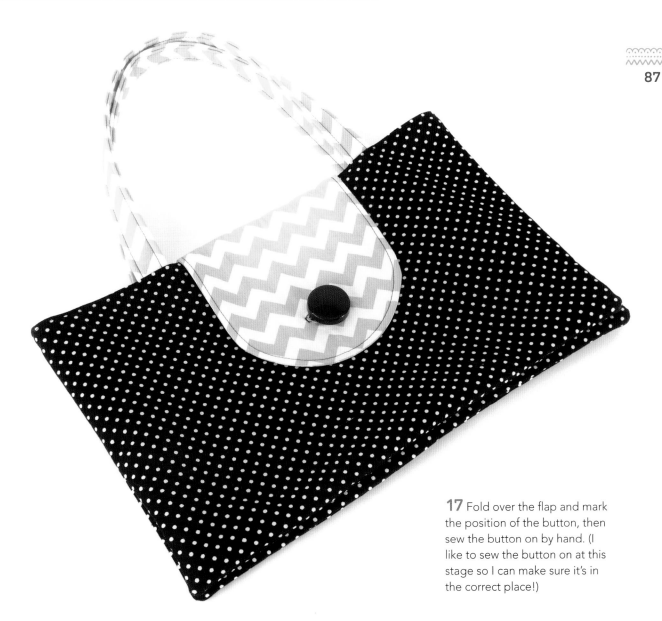

17 Fold over the flap and mark the position of the button, then sew the button on by hand. (I like to sew the button on at this stage so I can make sure it's in the correct place!)

BIG BOW TOTE

The pretty bow adds an element of fun to this chic, contemporary tote. I kept this one simple, but remember that you can add inside pockets and a zipped panel if you wish!

You will need

- 107 x 41cm (42 x 16in) outer fabric
- 107 x 56cm (42 x 22in) fabric for lining
- 86.5 x 30.5cm (34 x 12in) fusible fleece
- 4 buttons
- Strong wet fabric glue

Finished size

39.5 x 21.5 x 4cm (15½ x 8½ x 1½in), excluding handles

Using your templates

You will need to use the whole tote outline with small cut-out corners, the handle outline and the bow outline all from TEMPLATE 1. All templates should be placed on the fold of the fabric as indicated.

Template 1
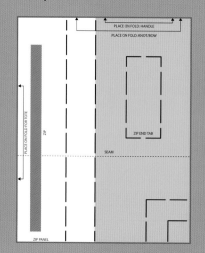

Template 1

Template 1
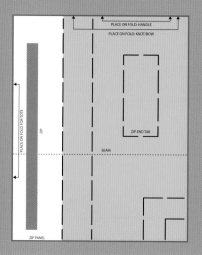

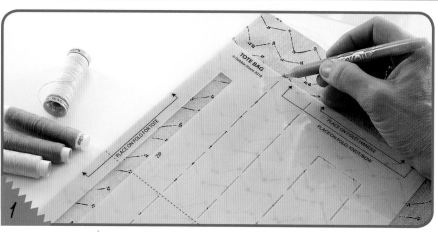

1 Place your tote template over the fold of fabric and draw around the outline with the small cut-out corners. Cut out two pieces of outer and two lining fabrics and fuse fleece to the wrong sides of the outer pieces.

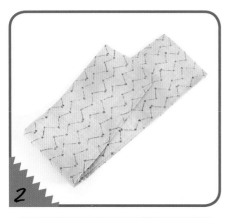 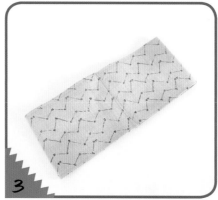 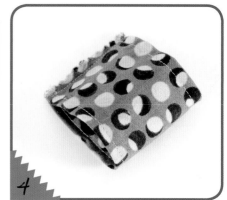

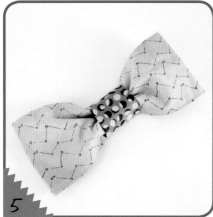 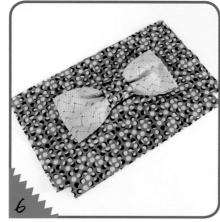 

2 Cut two pieces of lining fabric from the bow outline on your template. Sew the two pieces right sides together along the long sides to make a tube, turn right side out and press, then edge stitch along the seams.

3 Fold the two open ends to the centre and sew along the raw edges through all the layers with a close zigzag stitch.

4 Cut a piece of outer fabric measuring 15.25cm (6in) square. Fold two opposite sides wrong sides together to the centre and edge stitch along each side. Sew the two raw edges together to make a tube.

5 With the seam at the back, thread the lining bow fabric through this small tube until the tube sits centrally. Secure with a few spots of glue dotted inside the tube.

6 Place the bow on the centre of one of the outer tote pieces with the centre of the bow 11.5cm (4½in) from the top. Secure with a few hand stitches, or glue in place if you prefer.

7 Sew the two outer sections right sides together leaving the top and the cut-out corners unsewn. Pinch the cut-out corners so that the side seams sit on top of the base seam and sew to make the bag base squared off.

8 Cut two pieces of handle fabric using the template; adjust the length of the handles if you wish to make them longer or shorter. Make up two closed-ended handles following the instructions on page 19.

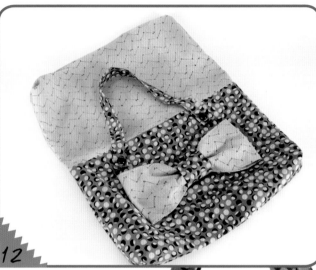

9 Pin the handles to the top of the outer bag pieces, 10cm (4in) from either side and 5cm (2in) from the top; angle the handle ends slightly so that they point towards the bottom corners. Secure with glue, then remove the pins. Hand-sew the buttons in place through the handles.

10 Sew the lining pieces right sides together, leaving the top and cut-out corners unsewn and leaving a turning gap of about 15.25cm (6in) in the bottom seam. Pinch the cut-out corners and sew to make the base squared off.

11 Drop the outer bag inside the lining with right sides together. Tuck the handles out of the way and sew around the top.

12 Turn right side out and sew the opening closed.

13 Push the lining inside the bag and press. Top-stitch around the top edge to complete.

A LITTLE EXTRA SOMETHING

Using the 15 designs as a starting point, it is simple to mix and match zips, appliqué, pockets, bows, fastenings and handles to create exactly the bag you want. But as well as this, here are a few ideas to get you started with *adapting* the templates to create bags that are different sizes and shapes.

- **Extend the lining** of your tote by adding 2.5cm (1in) to the top. As the lining will be longer than the outer fabric, it will create a decorative border around the top of your bag. You'll need to add a 2cm (¾in) strip of fusible fleece to the lining.

- **Make the straps longer** by adding a few extra inches to the template; cut the new strap from card to create an additional re-usable template.

- **Make** the base of your bag into a square to **create a storage tub**! Here's how to do it:

Here, I used a flap fastening but decorated the front with a small bow. I also added a few pockets to the lining to create a more versatile space. Think about what you will use the bag for and then consider what features you can add that will make the bag useful to you.

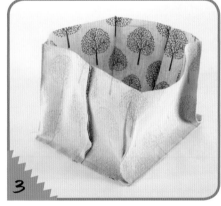

1 Draw around the tote template, but instead of cutting the 5cm (2in) squares from the bottom corners, cut 10cm (4in) squares. You'll need two outer pieces with fleece fused to the wrong sides, and two lining pieces.

2 Sew the outer pieces right sides together, leaving the cut-out corners and the top unsewn. Fold the cut-out corners so that the side seams sit over the bottom seam, and sew straight across. Turn right side out. To help make the cube rigid, crease the sides and base, then top-stitch along the creases on the right side.

3 Repeat with the lining, but this time don't turn right side out.

4 Drop the lining inside the cube, wrong sides facing, and tack/baste around the top edge. Finish the raw edge with bias binding (see pages 24–25).

This elegant tote features piping and
a magnetic fastening, as well as a
squared-off base. See pages 50–53.

This fun tote is constructed from patchworked fabric and closes with a button fastening. See pages 46–49.

INDEX